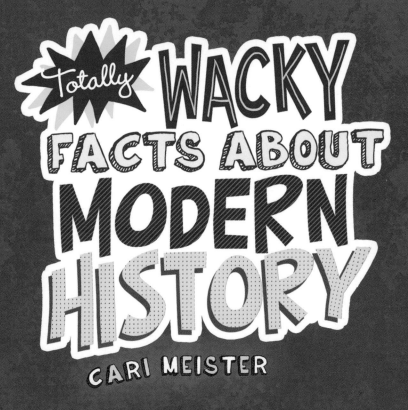

Totally WACKY FACTS ABOUT MODERN HISTORY

CARI MEISTER

CAPSTONE PRESS
a capstone imprint

QUEEN ELIZABETH I

of England had more than 2,000 dresses.

In 1571 Queen Elizabeth I decreed that **ALL MEN HAD TO WEAR HATS ON SUNDAYS.**

Elizabeth I is the only English queen who never married.

I just WANT A HUG!

A **HORDE** OF **RABBITS** ONCE ATTACKED THE FRENCH EMPEROR **NAPOLEON BONAPARTE.**

Napoleon suffered from **AILUROPHOBIA.** That means he was afraid of cats.

Napoleon didn't like his wife's name (Rose), so he changed it (to Josephine).

WINSTON CHURCHILL,
former prime minister of
GREAT BRITAIN,
was related to George Washington,
the first U.S. president.

Churchill loved his bed so much, he often held important meetings in his bedroom.

Churchill preferred **SLIP-ON SHOES** because he didn't like to waste time tying shoelaces.

ADOLF HITLER,

leader of Nazi Germany, was rejected from art school twice.

Hitler was so worried about being poisoned that he kept "food testers" on staff.

The famous magician **HARRY HOUDINI'S** first performance took place when he was just **9 YEARS OLD.**

In his first performance, Houdini picked up pins with his **EYELASHES!**

He made 35 cents for the performance.

When the pioneer pilot **AMELIA EARHART** was young, she had an imaginary Arabian horse named Saladin.

Earhart had her own aviation-inspired fashion line. It included blouses with propeller-shaped buttons.

In 1937 Amelia Earhart and her airplane disappeared over the Pacific Ocean.

GENGHIS KHAN
(1162–1227)
LEADER OF THE MONGOL EMPIRE

Genghis Khan conquered more than 12 million square miles (31 million square kilometers) of territory.

That's more than any other leader in history.

His death is a mystery.

Genghis Khan's legacy lives on—16 million direct descendants carry his genes today.

The famous Italian artist and inventor
LEONARDO DA VINCI
drew plans for "floating snowshoes."

Da Vinci could draw with one hand at the same time his other hand wrote backward.

Da Vinci was a very slow painter, and many of his paintings were never finished.

The famous physicist **ALBERT EINSTEIN** didn't start talking until he was 3 years old.

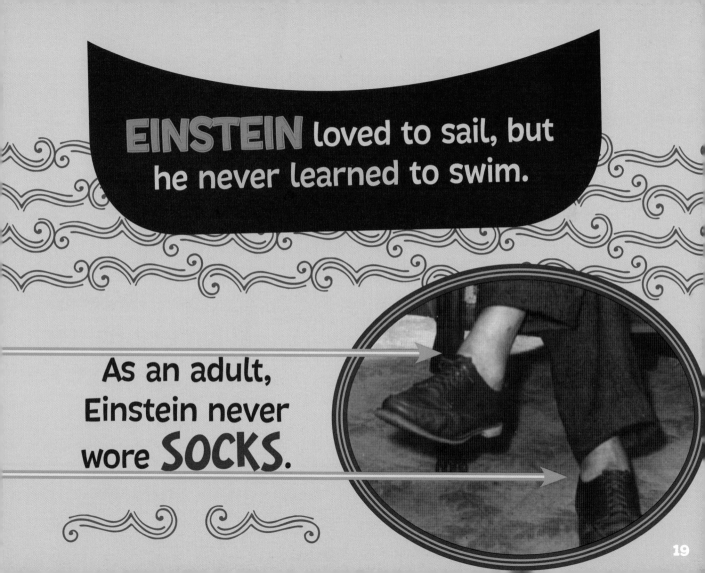

EINSTEIN loved to sail, but he never learned to swim.

As an adult, Einstein never wore **SOCKS**.

WOLFGANG MOZART, a famous composer, wrote music before he could write words.

MOZART wrote an entire symphony when he was only 8 years old.

Mozart's full name was

JOHANNES CHRYSOSTOMUS WOLFGANGUS THEOPHILUS MOZART.

AND NOW SOME WACKY FACTS
ABOUT U.S. PRESIDENTS:

JOHN ADAMS and Thomas Jefferson both died on July 4, 1826.

ULYSSES S. GRANT once got a speeding ticket for riding his horse too fast.

CALVIN COOLIDGE often had people rub Vaseline on his head while he ate breakfast in bed.

WOODROW WILSON painted his golf balls black so he could play in the snow.

The "S" in **HARRY S TRUMAN** does not stand for anything.

Six presidents have had the
first name
JAMES.

AND EVEN MORE ABOUT U.S. PRESIDENTS:

HERBERT HOOVER'S first
job was picking bugs
off of potato plants.

A family of plants was named after
THOMAS JEFFERSON.

ABRAHAM LINCOLN was a licensed bartender.

Most pirates didn't make captives **"WALK THE PLANK."** They just threw them overboard.

BLACKBEARD'S pirate ship was found off the coast of North Carolina, USA, in 1996. The ship was loaded with cannons.

SMALL FEET

were considered **beautiful** in China, so parents would "bind" a daughter's feet to stunt their growth.

Some Europeans used to paint fake veins on their faces to make them look pale.

People used to whiten their skin with lead, which made their hair fall out.

WACKY HAIRSTYLES

"The Beehive," circa the 1950s

Japanese samurai "Chronmage," circa 12th –19th centuries

Monks "Tonsure," circa Medieval Europe

"The Hedgehog," circa 1776

I decree
NO NAP TIMES
EVER!

LOUIS XIV
was 4 years old
when he became
king of France.

MARY, QUEEN OF SCOTS, became queen when her father died. She was 6 days old!

PU-YI, the last emperor of China, came to power when he was 2 years old.

SULTAN ISMAIL of Morocco (1672–1727) had more than 1,000 children!

I bet he won't **REMEMBER ALL OUR BIRTHDAYS!**

An **18th century** Russian woman had **69 CHILDREN!**

16 PAIRS OF TWINS

7 SETS OF TRIPLETS

AND

4 SETS OF QUADRUPLETS.

WORLD WAR I (1914–1918):

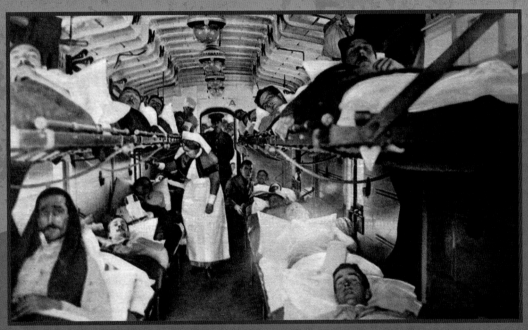

When Germans ran out of linen for bandages,
they used lace curtains instead.

SPIES WROTE MESSAGES ON THE BACKS OF BUTTONS.

On CHRISTMAS DAY, 1914, GERMAN and BRITISH soldiers STOPPED FIGHTING and played SOCCER together.

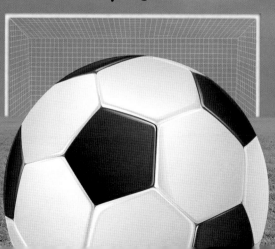

WORLD WAR I (1914–1918):

TANKS were originally called "landships."

The BRITISH used the word "TANK" to TRICK their enemies into THINKING the vehicles were only WATER TANKS.

The first **SUBMARINE**
was called
"THE TURTLE"
and was used in the
**AMERICAN
REVOLUTIONARY
WAR.**

During the **REVOLUTIONARY WAR, GEORGE WASHINGTON,** called a ceasefire to return his enemy's **LOST DOG.**

MYTHS ABOUT U.S. PRESIDENT GEORGE WASHINGTON, EXPOSED!

His dentures were
NOT MADE OF WOOD.
They were made from a **combination** of
HIPPO IVORY and HORSE,
HUMAN, and DONKEY TEETH.

HE NEVER CUT DOWN
A CHERRY TREE.

THROUGHOUT HISTORY,

MANY THINGS WERE USED TO MAKE FALSE TEETH.

INCLUDING:

WOOD

ROCKS

IVORY

SEASHELLS

BONE

ANIMAL TEETH

From the
MEDIEVAL
Gross Files

People in medieval Europe drank
GOLD POWDER
mixed with water to relieve
sore muscles.

A medieval feast might include "BLACKBIRD PIE" or vulture.

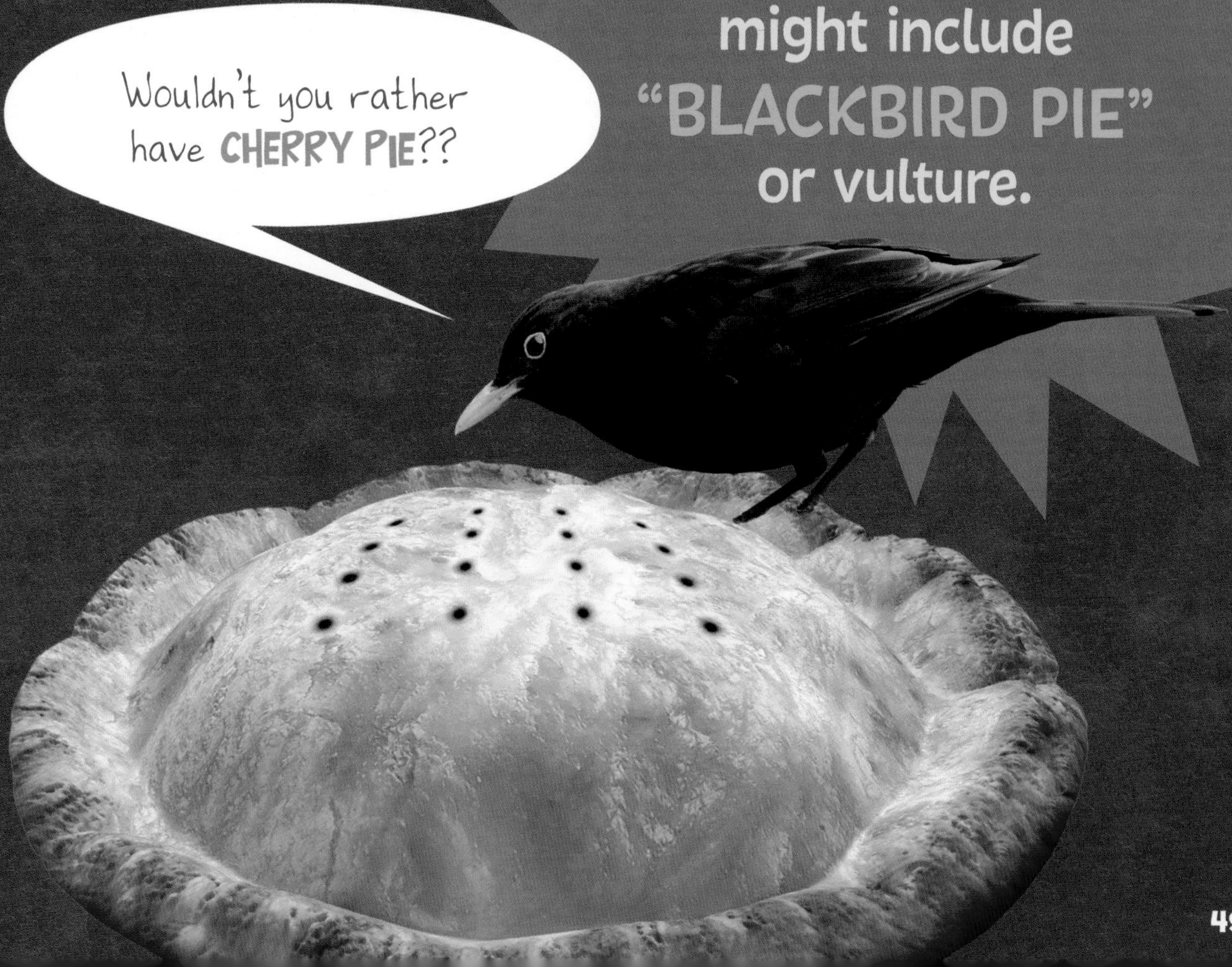

The Chinese invented **TOILET PAPER** in the year 851 CE.

Other things people have used **TO WIPE THEIR BEHINDS:** rose petals, leaves, straw, rags, pages from catalogs or books, corncobs.

LEECHES have been used in medicine for more than 3,000 years.

Leeches were put over an affected area to suck out "bad" blood.

During the 1830s in France, more than 35 million leeches were used in medicinal treatments PER YEAR!

Once a Parisian leech collector fell asleep and woke up to find himself completely covered in leeches!

But I LIKE my HEAD!

KING CHARLES

I was BEHEADED for being a traitor.

Out of **RESPECT** for the royal family, his head was later **SEWN BACK ON.**

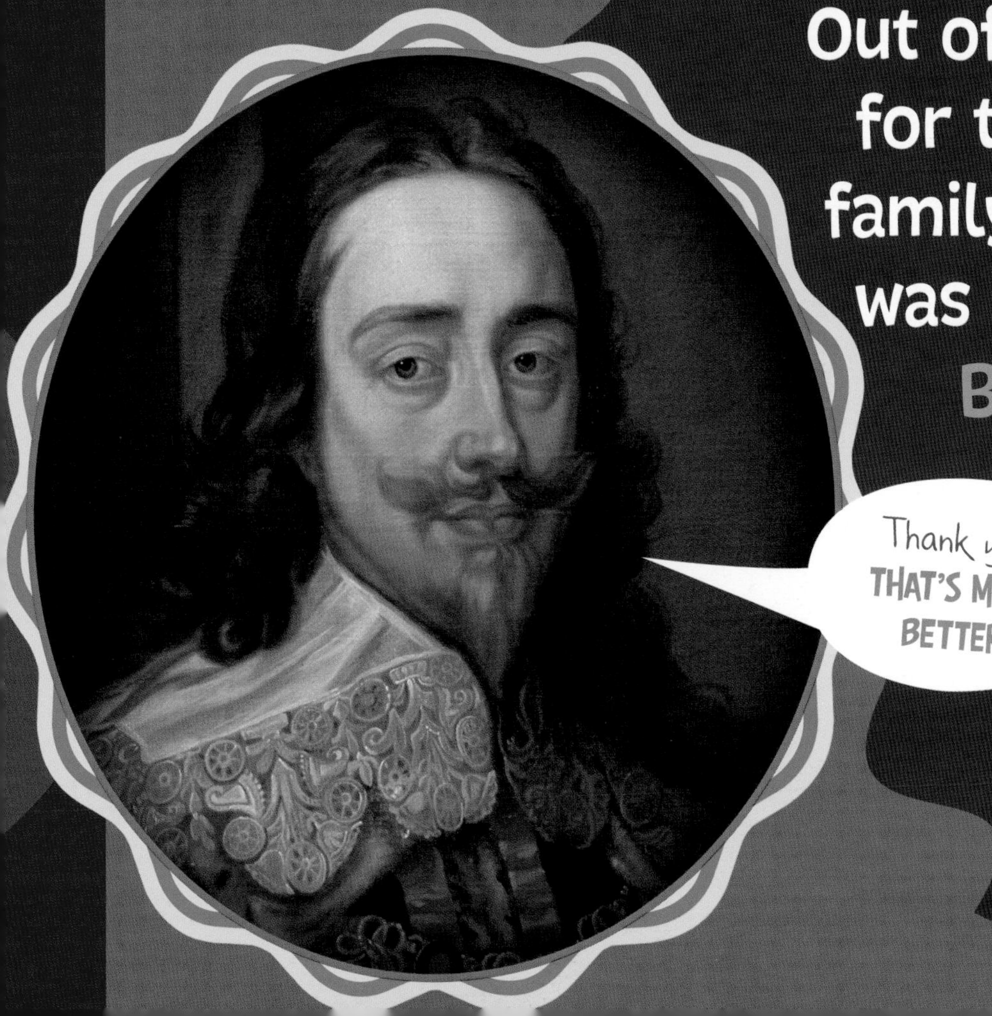

KING LOUIS XIII

of France suffered from BALDNESS, so he started a trend of wearing BIG, CURLY WIGS.

The trend spread to **CHARLES II**, the king of England at the time.

It is still common for **JUDGES** in England to wear **WIGS**.

JAPANESE SAMURAI had SOCKS with a SEPARATE PLACE for the BIG TOES.

The average SAMURAI stood only about 5 FEET, 4 INCHES (1.63 METERS) TALL.

SAMURAI were trained in BATTLE TACTICS, SWORDSMANSHIP, and POETRY.

VIKINGS bathed about ONCE A WEEK— way more OFTEN than most PEOPLE OF THE DAY.

What did Vikings do for fun? **THEY SKIED!**

Contrary to popular belief, **VIKINGS** DID NOT WEAR HORNS on their helmets.

To navigate the ocean, **VIKINGS** used **CRYSTALS.**

VIKINGS buried their dead in boats.

THE RMS TITANIC

The **TITANIC'S ANCHOR** weighed more than 15 tons (14 metric tons). **TWENTY HORSES HAD TO CARRY IT TO THE SHIPYARD!**

The last
meal for the
Titanic's first class
passengers
included
11 COURSES!

After the
Titanic sank,
ROWS OF
UNBROKEN
CHINA PLATES
rested on the
ocean floor.

ESSEX

In 1820 the 238-ton (216-metric-ton) whaling ship **ESSEX** capsized after being rammed twice by a **SPERM WHALE.**

The FEW SURVIVORS drifted on the sea in small boats for 94 DAYS BEFORE RESCUED.

Herman Melville's novel *MOBY DICK* was inspired by the harrowing tale.

HINDENBURG

The airship **HINDENBURG** had a PIANO, a DINING ROOM, and a SMOKING ROOM on board.

AIRSHIPS, INCLUDING THE HINDENBURG, WERE ABOUT 750-800 FEET (229-244 METERS) LONG. THAT'S ABOUT AS LONG AS TWO AND A HALF FOOTBALL FIELDS.

D-LZ129

The *Hindenburg* **EXPLODED** in 1937. No one knows why.

COOL JOBS OF THE PAST

A **RESURRECTIONIST** snatched bodies from graves and sold them to medical schools.

When digging a body from a grave, a **RESURRECTIONIST** used a **WOODEN SHOVEL** so it wouldn't make any noise.

BODY SNATCHING was so common in the 17th century that people started to bury their dead in metal, cage-like caskets.

MORE COOL JOBS

KNOCKER-UPPERS tapped on windows with large poles or shot peas out of straws to wake up factory workers.

THE GROOM OF THE STOOL wiped a king's behind after he used the toilet.

A **DOG WHIPPER** kept dogs quiet in the churchyard.

ROYAL RAT CATCHERS CAUGHT RATS.

Rat Catcher John Newton could catch up to 340 RATS in one night at Windsor Castle!

If you lived in the 17th century and you wanted to insult a man's intelligence you would call him a

"wattlehead."

Throughout history, **LAZY PEOPLE** have been called

BED-PRESSERS, LOLL-POOPS, AND LOITERSACKS.

THE WORD "POOP" WAS NOT USED UNTIL AROUND 1900.

INSTEAD,
THE BRITISH USED:

NIGHT SOIL—poop removed from European cities at night

GONG—a historical word for poop

THREE THINGS
most **SEA-FARING COLONISTS**
had in common:

HEAD LICE

BIG DREAMS

BODY LICE

KRISTI YAMAGUCHI, 1992 Olympic gold medalist figure skater, was born with **DEFORMED FEET.**

After contracting POLIO as a child and spending YEARS IN A LEG BRACE, **WILMA RUDOLPH** went on to win 3 GOLD MEDALS in track and field in the 1960 OLYMPICS.

South African swimmer **NATALIE DU TOIT** competed in the 2008 Beijing Olympics with an AMPUTATED LEG AND NO PROSTHESIS.

LONGEST TENNIS MATCH:

11 hours over a stretch of 3 days
THEY PLAYED 183 GAMES TOTAL!
(Isner vs. Mahut, 2010)

THE LONGEST BASKETBALL GAME

HAD SIX OVERTIMES!

Indianapolis Olympians
vs.
Rochester Royals, 1951

Romanian President *Nicolae Ceaușescu* banned the board game

SCRABBLE.

In 2011 the Malaysian government banned people from wearing **YELLOW**.

Since 1992 it has been illegal to chew **GUM** in Singapore.

For over 200 years, it was illegal in France for women to wear **PANTS** in public.

In 2012
KING RICHARD III's
body was found under a parking lot in England.

From the 16th through the 19th centuries, DECEASED MONKS IN PALERMO, ITALY, were mummified, dressed, and put on display.

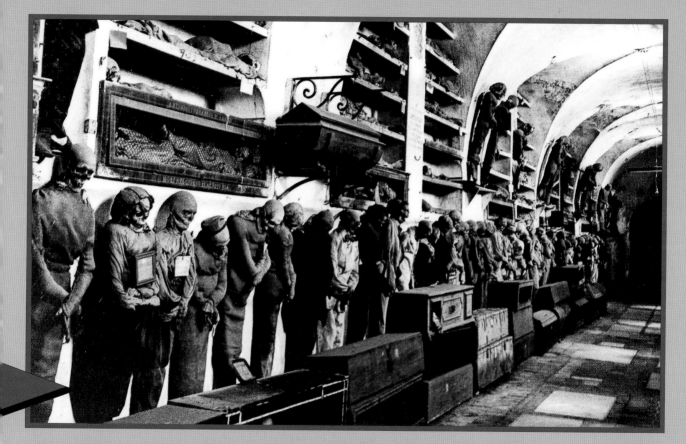

Today, tourists can visit the Palermo, Italy, monks at the Catacombs of the Capuchins.

THE INCA PEOPLE

from South America used **LLAMA DUNG** for fuel.

EARLY AMERICAN PIONEERS
burned dried buffalo poop to keep warm.

PIANO KEYS

were once made from elephant and walrus tusks.

In the 1800s, **WHALE PARTS** were used to make **CORSETS.**

The Catholic Pope **LEO X** had a pet **WHITE ELEPHANT** named Hanno.

Napoleon's wife had a **PET ORANGUTAN** that enjoyed dining on turnips.

Your mustache is TICKLING MY EAR!

The Spanish artist **SALVADOR DALÌ** would take his pet ocelot, **BABOU**, out to eat.

MOZART
held a FUNERAL
when his
PET BIRD died.

U.S. president **ANDREW JACKSON** loved his **PARROT** so much that it was invited to his **FUNERAL.**

A mythical
triangle called the

BERMUDA TRIANGLE

covers more than
500,000 square miles
(1,294,994 square kilometers)
of ocean just off the
southeastern coast
of Florida.

More than
100 STRANGE HAPPENINGS
have been reported in the
BERMUDA TRIANGLE.

On December 5, 1945,
five U.S. Navy bombers
VANISHED INTO THIN AIR
over the BERMUDA TRIANGLE

In 1924 a **CAR** in the United States

COST ABOUT $295.00.

$295.00

THE FIRST SEATBELTS

were not put into cars until the 1950s.

Car seats for babies were not widely used in the United States until the 1980s.

THE FIRST COMPUTERS WERE GIGANTIC. THEY OFTEN FILLED ENTIRE ROOMS!

The first COMPUTER MOUSE had a wooden shell and two wheels.

THE APOLLO 11 MISSION USED COMPUTERS less powerful than your CELL PHONE!

The first **KENTUCKY FRIED CHICKEN** restaurant was inside a GAS STATION.

TACO BELL—today a billion-dollar business—started out as a HOT DOG STAND.

The first **McDonald's** restaurant served peanut butter and jelly sandwiches.

THE FIRST HOLLYWOOD MOVIE

(made in 1910) only took **TWO DAYS** to film.

In the 1970s movie *THE SWARM,* the studio used **22 MILLION LIVE BEES.**

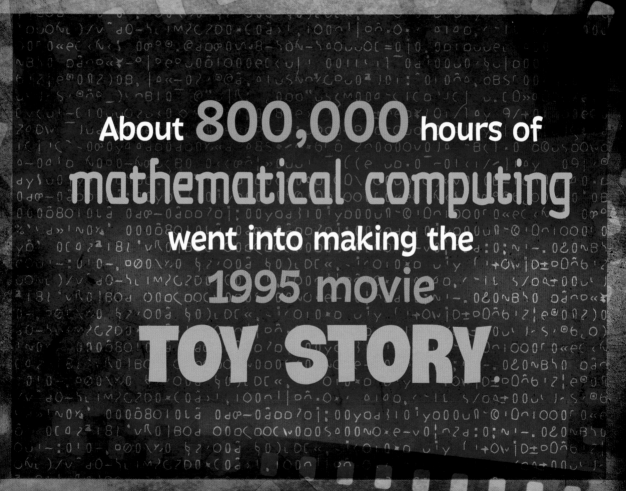

About **800,000** hours of **mathematical computing** went into making the 1995 movie **TOY STORY**

THE TATOOINE SCENES
in the **STAR WARS** movies were filmed in Tunisia, Africa.

If you visit **TUNISIA,** you can actually stay in **LUKE SKYWALKER'S** home. It's a **HOTEL** now.

In 1967 Canada built a

UFO LANDING PAD

TO WELCOME ALIENS. So far

NO ALIENS HAVE USED IT.

GLOSSARY

aviation—having to do with the flying, development, or business of aircraft

capsize—when a boat turns over in the water

ceasefire—to stop fighting a war for a specific period of time

decree—an official order

descendant—a person related to someone from the past

monastery—a place where monks work and live

polio—a disease that affects the nerves; it often makes people unable to walk.

prime minister—in some places in the world, a prime minister is the head of government

propellers—blades that (when spinning) help an aircraft fly

samurai—a warrior from Japan

READ MORE

Davis, Todd, and Marc Frey. *The New Big Book of U.S Presidents*. Philadelphia: Running Press Kids, 2013.

Gitlin, Marty. *The Totally Gross History of Medieval Europe*. Totally Gross History. New York: The Rosen Publishing Group, Inc., 2016.

Lee, Adrienne. *Samurai*. Legendary Warriors. North Mankato, Minn.: Capstone Press, 2015.

Senior, Kathryn. *You Wouldn't Want to be Sick in the 16th Century!* Danbury, CT: Children's Press, 2014.

INTERNET SITES

FactHound offers a safe, fun way to find Internet sites related to this book. All of the sites on FactHound have been researched by our staff.

Here's all you do:

Visit *www.facthound.com*

Type in this code: 9781491483862

INDEX

Mind Benders are published by Capstone,
1710 Roe Crest Drive, North Mankato, Minnesota 56003
www.capstonepub.com

Editor: Megan Atwood
Designer: Veronica Scott
Media Researcher: Jo Miller
Production Specialist: Gene Bentdahl

Library of Congress Cataloging-in-Publication Data
Names: Meister, Cari, author.
Title: Totally wacky facts about modern history / by Cari Meister.
Description: North Mankato, Minnesota : Capstone Press, 2017. | Series: Mind benders |
Includes bibliographical references and index. | Audience: Ages 8–12. | Audience: Grades 4 to 6.
Identifiers: LCCN 2016010225| ISBN 9781491483862 (library binding) |
ISBN 9781491483886 (pbk.) | ISBN 9781491483909 (ebook (pdf) |
Subjects: LCSH: History, Modern--Juvenile literature. | History, Modern--Miscellanea--Juvenile literature. |
Curiosities and wonders--Juvenile literature.
Classification: LCC D208 .M45 2017 | DDC 909.08--dc23
LC record available at http://lccn.loc.gov/2016010225

Photo Credits
Alamy: Chronicle, 30, dieKleinert, 97, INTERFOTO, 67, North Wind Picture Archives, 3; AP Images: Alastair Grant, File, 82, (front); Bridgeman Images: Private Collection/Photo © O. Vaering, 61, Corbis: Jason Hawkes, 73, (castle), Underwood & Underwood, 24, (Woodrow Wilson); Getty Images: Bettmann, 7, Hulton Archive/Three Lions/Lucien Aigner, 18, 19, Print Collector/Ann Ronan Pictures, 23; Newscom: akg-images, 58, 79, 95 (Andrew Jackson), akg-images/Andre Held, 34, Cultura/George Karbus Photography, 66, Design Pics, 35, (right), Design Pics/Steve Nagy, 108-109, Everett Collection, 10, 80, (right), 91, 93, 98, 103, Florilegius/Album, 33, (left), Glasshouse Images/Manning de V. Lee, 62, Icon SMI/Manny Millan, 80, (left), Ingram Publishing, 84, REX/Mark Pain, 81, UIG National Trust, 54, 55, 57, (left), World History Archive, (left), 68-69, (airship), ZUMA Press/Glen Stubbe, 45, ZUMA Press/Mark Richards, 100, ZUMA Press/Ropi/Antonio Pisacreta, 87; Shutterstock: Adwo, 15, albund, 82, (background), 49, (pie), Algol, 63, Amy Johansson, 28 (plank), Andrey_Kuzmin, 29, (porthole), Art Konovalov, 9, Asaf Eliason, 11 (both), bikeriderlondon, 36-37, camilla$$, back cover, Christos Georghiou, 101, Creative Travel Projects, 24, (background), cynoclub, 95 (parrot), dedMazay, 70, Dobrynina Elena, 42, Eka Panova, 31 (all), Elle Arden Images, 12, Eric Isselee, 43, Everett Historical, cover (tank), 2, 8, 13, 16, 27, 29, (pirate), 38, 40, 64, exopixel, 51, (corn cob), Georgios Kollidas, 44, GreenBelka, 96, gst, 102, (left), jaylopez, 105, Joshua Rainey Photography, 88, Kristen Smith, 32, (left), Lena_graphics, cover, (alien), Lightspring, 83, Luca Nichetti, 49, (bird), Magdanatka, 51, (rose petals), Marques, 106-107, Marzolino, 20, Marzolino, 32, (right), Oliver Hoffmann, 102, (right), PathDoc, 74, PathDoc, 75, patrimonio designs ltd, cover, (samurai), Pelevina Ksinia, 73, (rat), PhotoTodos, 51, (book), Protasov AN, 78, 79, scimmery, 5, Sergiu Ungureanu, 24, (golf ball), sharpner, 57, (right), Studio_smile, 28-29, Sudowoodo, cover, (poop), Sudowoodo, 76, 77, sydeen, 52, TaMaNKunG, 39, (background), The_Pixel, 68-69, (football fields), vasosh, 39, (soccer ball), vitmark, 88-89, Wallenrock, 4, SuperStock: Science and Society, 71, Wikimedia: Carlo Crivelli, 33, (right)

Design Elements by Capstone and Shutterstock

Printed in the United States of America.
032016   009689F16